TRICERATOPS

by Bradley Cole

D1092006

Cody Koala

An Imprint of Pop!
popbooksonline.com

abdobooks.com
Published by Pop!, a division of ABDO, PO Box 398166, Minneapolis, Minnesota 55439. Copyright © 2019 by POP, LLC. International copyrights reserved in all countries. No part of this book may be reproduced in any form without written permission from the publisher. Pop!™ is a trademark and logo of POP, LLC.

Printed in the United States of America, North Mankato, Minnesota.

082018
012019

THIS BOOK CONTAINS RECYCLED MATERIALS

Cover Photo: iStockphoto
Interior Photos: iStockphoto, 1; Roger Hall/Science Source, 4–5; Mark Hallett Paleoart/Science Source, 7; Shutterstock Images, 9 (top), 9 (bottom left); Colin Keates/Dorling Kindersley/Natural History Museum, London/Science Source, 9 (bottom right); Millard H. Sharp/Science Source, 11; The Natural History Museum, London/Science Source, 12, 19; Richard Bizley/Science Source, 15; Francois Gohier/Science Source, 17; De Agostini Picture Library/Science Source, 20

Editor: Meg Gaertner
Series Designer: Laura Mitchell

Library of Congress Control Number: 2018949753
Publisher's Cataloging-in-Publication Data
Names: Cole, Bradley, author.
Title: Triceratops / by Bradley Cole.
Description: Minneapolis, Minnesota : Pop!, 2019 | Series: Dinosaurs | Includes online resources and index.
Identifiers: ISBN 9781532161827 (lib. bdg.) | ISBN 9781641855532 (pbk) | ISBN 9781532162886 (ebook)
Subjects: LCSH: Triceratops--Juvenile literature. | Dinosaurs--Juvenile literature. | Extinct animals--Juvenile literature.
Classification: DDC 567.915--dc23

Hello! My name is

Cody Koala

Pop open this book and you'll find QR codes like this one, loaded with information, so you can learn even more!

Scan this code* and others like it while you read, or visit the website below to make this book pop.

popbooksonline.com/triceratops

*Scanning QR codes requires a web-enabled smart device with a QR code reader app and a camera.

Table of Contents

Chapter 1

Giant Plant Eater

Triceratops was a

plant-eating dinosaur.

It walked on four legs.

It lived 67 million years ago.

This was during the late

Cretaceous Period.

Watch a video here!

Triceratops grew to be as long as two cars together. It was almost twice as tall as an adult human. It weighed as much as an adult elephant.

The name Triceratops means "three-horned face."

Chapter 2

Three-Horned Face

Triceratops had three horns on its **skull**. Two long horns were above its eyes. One short horn was above its mouth.

Complete an activity here!

Triceratops had a large curve of bone that grew from the back of its head. It is called the frill. The frill may have protected the dinosaur's neck from **predators**.

Triceratops had a parrot-like beak. It also had lots of sharp teeth. It ate plants such as ferns.

Triceratops had one of the largest skulls of any land animal.

Cretaceous Life

Triceratops used its horns to fight. It fought off predators such as Tyrannosaurus rex. The horns also helped Triceratops attract a **mate**.

Learn more here!

Fossil Clues

Scientists have found Triceratops **fossils** across western North America. These fossils give scientists clues about how the dinosaur lived.

Learn more here!

For a long time, scientists thought Triceratops lived alone its whole life. The known fossils were all of individual Triceratops.

Then scientists found the fossils of three young Triceratops together. Scientists think young Triceratops traveled together for protection.

More than 50 Triceratops skulls have been discovered.

Making Connections

Text-to-Self

Have you ever seen a dinosaur fossil in a museum? If yes, what did you think? If no, would you want to? Why or why not?

Text-to-Text

Have you read other books about dinosaurs? How were those dinosaurs similar to or different from Triceratops?

Text-to-World

Why do you think scientists study fossils to learn about dinosaurs?

Glossary

Cretaceous Period – a period that lasted from about 145 million years ago to 66 million years ago.

fossil – the remains of a plant or an animal from a long time ago.

mate – an animal that is paired with another animal for having babies.

predator – an animal that hunts other animals.

skull – the framework of bone that forms a human's or animal's head.

Index

Online Resources

popbooksonline.com

Thanks for reading this Cody Koala book!

Scan this code* and others like it in this book, or visit the website below to make this book pop!

popbooksonline.com/triceratops

*Scanning QR codes requires a web-enabled smart device with a QR code reader app and a camera.